Animal Tracks

Wild Poems to Read Aloud

by Charles Ghigna
illustrated by John Speirs

Harry N. Abrams, Inc., Publishers

ELEPHANT BATH

Some elephants like to bathe
Hour after hour,
While others like to fill their trunks
And give themselves a shower!

PIGS

Pigs are playful.
Pigs are pink.
Pigs are smarter
Than you think.

Pigs are pudgy.
Pigs are plump.
Pigs can run
But never jump.

Pigs are loyal.
Pigs are true.
Pigs don't care
For barbecue.

HIPPOS

Hippos swim.
Hippos snort.
Hippo legs
Are rather short.

Hippo ears
Are pink and tiny.
Hippo hide
Is very shiny.

Hippo tails
Are stout and stubby.
Hippo hips are
Kind of chubby.

Hippos stay
Rather quiet.
Hippos never
Like to diet.

WHAT'S INSIDE A CAMEL'S HUMP?

What's inside a camel's hump?
A bowling ball? An old tree stump?
A turtle shell? A bicycle pump?
Jumping beans that lost their jump?
I've never seen such a curious lump.
Maybe it's just a big goose bump!

PENGUINS

Penguins waddle.
Penguins stroll
All around
The cold South Pole.

Penguins slide.
Penguins swim.
Penguins never
Look too slim.

Penguins play.
Penguins dress
Always in
Their Sunday best.

TURTLES

Turtles sit.
Turtles wait.
Turtles never
Think they're late.

Turtles crawl.
Turtles snap.
Turtles take
A long, long nap.

Turtles listen.
Turtles hide.
Turtles like
To stay inside.

I'M NOT LION

No matter how hard I look,
I've never seen a worm inside a book.

Is this stuff all well known?
I've never seen a shark who made a loan.

This, too, sounds rather rash,
I've never seen a cow who carries cash.

I may be out to lunch,
I've never seen a rabbit throw
     a punch.

I hate to be a bore,
I've never seen a wolf at any door.

Is all this one big joke?
I've never seen a pig inside a poke.

I may be getting this too slowly,
I've never seen a mackerel who was holy.

THE ARMADILLO

Someone played
An awful prank;
They turned a mole
Into a tank!

EYE SPY

Tarantulas have six small eyes
To see around the room,
While bumblebees have five bright eyes
To see into each bloom.

Most creatures only have two eyes,
Though you may wonder then
Why horses have a pair of eyes—
While horseshoe crabs have ten!

THE HUNGRY GOAT

He ate a can of peppers.
He ate a can of prunes.
We haven't seen that hungry goat
In many, many moons!

DO NOT BULLY A BULL

Do not badger a badger.
Do not bully a bull.
Do not beep at the long-horned sheep,
Especially while wearing wool!

A BATCH
OF BEASTS

A cast of hawks,
A knot of toads,
A troop of kangaroo;

These are the names
Of wild groups
When there are more than two.

A husk of hare,
A trip of goats,
A watch of nightingale,

A route of wolves,
A charm of finch,
A covey of young quail.

A shoal of bass,
A drove of cows,
A sounder of the swine;

These are the names
Of groups of beasts
When two or more combine.

DOGS MAKE ME SMILE

Dogs make me smile,
Hanging out of SUVs,
Riding on the summer breeze.

Dogs make me smile,
With floppy ears and rubber noses,
They ride the wind in drooling poses.

Dogs make me smile,
Flying by in cars and trucks.
I wonder if they think they're ducks?

PET NAMES

We call the cat a kitty.
We call the dog a mutt.
We call the pig a piggy.
We call the donkey—what?!

We call the vulture buzzard,
The pill bug, roly-poly.
We call the rabbit bunny,
As we pet it very slowly.

The animals and insects
Must think we are insane.
They'd like to give us all pet names,
But they are more humane!

WILD SYMPHONY

The clarinet looks like a snake,
The saxophone, a swan.
The piano's a smiling hippo,
The tuba, an elephant's yawn.

The bass looks like a grizzly bear,
Cymbals, like a clam.
The drum looks like a turtle,
The bagpipe, like a lamb.

A wild little symphony,
A beastly little band
Of animals and instruments
From kaZOO to baby grand!

DUCKS QUACK ME UP

Little duckies in the sun,
I like to see you having fun.

Little duckies on the lake,
I like to hear the noise you make.

Little duckies in a row,
Dinner's waiting just below.

Little duckies, when you sup
You always turn your bottoms up.

I JUST SAW A MOUSE

I just saw a mouse,
A very big mouse,
A scary mean mouse,
I did.

I jumped in the bed
And covered my head—
I wonder where HE
May have hid?

I WOULDN'T PET ON IT

We've got a squirrel in the attic.
We've got a robin in the eave.
We've got a chipmunk in the garden.
We've got pets you won't believe.

We've got a collie in the carport
And a kitten in the house.
We've got bunnies in the basement,
And, yes, we've got a mouse.

We've got parakeets and goldfish.
We've got turtles in the pond.
We've got gerbils in the bathroom
And a guinea pig named Ron.

We've got an ant farm in the bedroom
And a pregnant Peekapoo.
We've got most every animal,
But—we're going to the ZOO!

A POSSUM IN THE HOUSE

A possum got inside the house.
I thought it was a giant mouse.

It ran and hid beneath the bed
And then pretended he was dead.

I waited by the bedroom door.
The possum ran across the floor.

Possums look a lot like rats,
Except they are the size of cats.

With fifty teeth inside a snout,
It's always best to let them out.

THE MISSING SOUND

I like to listen to the sounds
Of every kind of bird,
Of every kind of animal
And insect that I've heard.

I've listened to some wild sounds
Like buzz and hiss and clop,
But one sound that I've never heard—
A weasel that goes pop!

THE BUTTERFLY AND
THE HUMMINGBIRD

See the little butterfly.
See it as it flutters by
Floating on the morning breeze
In and out beneath the trees.

See the little hummingbird.
The softest sound you ever heard.
See it as it starts to zoom
In and out of every bloom.

FROG ON A LOG

Hey, big old frog
On that small log.

Now don't you cough
Or you'll fall off.

You coughed! Oh no!
I toad you so.

THE SNAIL

Though he has no hands,
Only a tail,
Do not pity the lowly snail.

Though he has no pencil,
Or pen,
He leaves a message wherever he's been.

FLY SWATTER

The house is full of flies again.
I swat them for a penny
Until there aren't any.
Then I open the door—for more.

DREAM BOAT

If I could build a sailing ship,
And I could have one wish,
I'd want my helpers all to be
Dolphins, whales, and fish.

The sawfish would saw all the boards
And cut the mast and rails.
The shark known as the hammerhead,
Of course, would drive the nails.

For lights I'd use, if it agrees,
The bright electric eel.
The dolphin with its dorsal fin
Would be the sailboat's keel.

I'd ask the sailfish if it minds
Serving as the sail.
And for the anchor I would need
The giant humpback whale.

The captain of the sailing ship
(If I could have my wish),
Would be the one who sails the best—
The clever pilotfish.

WILD ROMANCE

I love EWE.

I'm not LION.

I really GOPHER you.

I never GNU this would happen.

You are so DEER to me.

It's more than I can BEAR.

Let us SEAL our love with a kiss.

I will always BEE yours.

I will never have any EGRETS.

You are my one and only GULL.

OWL always love you.

BIRDS IN THE SNOW

We scatter seeds upon the snow
And watch the snowbirds eat.
They leave a trail of little stars
Beneath their tiny feet.

THE SANDPIPER

Running up and down the beach
Beside the setting sun,
The piper paces back and forth
When each new day is done.

He bows his head and takes a drink
With his slender beak
Until a wave comes up to play
A game of hide-and-seek.

He hurries home along the shore
And spreads his wings in flight.
He calls back to his friend the sea
And wishes her good night.

SEAGULLS

No one knows the reason why
But when you look them in the eye
Seagulls turn and wave good-bye;

Unless you have an Oreo
And hold it up on tippy toe—
That's when they turn and wave hello!

A SNOWY DAY IN
THE EVERGLADES

I had a dream it snowed last night
Across the Everglades,
And all the gators marched around
In snowy big parades.

Each wore a funny crimson cap
Upon their gator heads,
And when they slid down marshy slopes,
Their bellies became sleds.

They made a snowman in the swamp
Whose tail was big and white.
They made snow angels in the snow
And had a snowball fight.

They raced out to the frozen lake
To pick some everblades,
And when they strapped them on their feet—
Ice gators in the 'Glades!

WHAT DOES A HOUND DOG DO ALL DAY?

He sleeps. He eats. He chases flies.
He looks for pheasant in the skies.

He barks. He growls. And then he snores.
He wakes and begs for out-of-doors.

He hunts. He howls. He loves kind words.
(He won't admit he's scared of birds.)

He runs. He jumps. He fetches sticks.
He finds your face and then he licks.

He gets his pets. He gets his pats.
He gets his kicks from chasing cats.

He sniffs. He tracks. He likes to roam.
He finds your lap when you are home.

WHAT WOULD
I LIKE TO DO?

I'd like to share this day with you.
I'd like to take us to the zoo.
I'd like to see the kangaroo.
I'd like to hear the pigeons coo.

I'd like to see the kinkajou.
I'd like to hear the kittens mew.
I'd like to see the baby gnu.
I'd like to hear the cattle moo.

I'd like to see the woolly ewe.
I'd like to hear the cockatoo.
And when we're through at the zoo—
I'd like to share tomorrow, too.

INDEX OF ANIMALS MENTIONED IN TEXT

ARTIST'S NOTE

I look to the freedom of line and luminous watercolor washes to bring out the high spirits and idiosyncrasies of the creatures that populate *Animal Tracks*. The drawings are first made using a Japanese HB mechanical pencil. When I'm ready to paint, I use a large selection of old dinner plates as my palette for mixing colors, which also makes my working space look like I am about to throw a dinner party! I always use Pelican Transparent Watercolor paints, Winsor and Newton Series 7 sable brushes sizes 0–2, and white gouache paint on Sanders Waterford "NOT" paper. I work lying on the floor before a large light box (which I use to trace my initial drawings onto the final paper), usually in the company of one of my cats, which might explain the occasional black hair to be found somewhere in my art.   —J. S.

For Benjamin Levaton —C. G.

A hearty thanks to Howard Reeves and Linas Alsenas for helping tame these wild beasts.   —C. G.

Designer: Edward Miller

Library of Congress Cataloging-in-Publication Data
Ghigna, Charles.
Animal tracks : more silly poems to read aloud / by Charles Ghigna ;
illustrated by John Speirs.
p. cm.
Summary: A collection of simple poems about such animals as lions,
hummingbirds, dogs, alligators, and seagulls.
ISBN 0-8109-4841-9
1. Animals—Juvenile poetry. 2. Children's poetry, American. [1.
Animals—Poetry. 2. American poetry.] I. Speirs, John, ill. II. Title.

PS3557.H5A8 2004
811'.54—dc22
2003014053

Printed and bound in the U.S.A.
10 9 8 7 6 5 4 3 2

ABRAMS
Harry N. Abrams, Inc.
100 Fifth Avenue
New York, N.Y. 10011
www.abramsbooks.com

Abrams is a subsidiary of LA MARTINIÈRE
GROUPE